Breathing Space

A Respite for Ministry Leaders

Eric D Willis

Breathing Space: A Respite for Ministry Leaders
Copyright © 2015 by Eric D. Willis

All rights reserved. No part of this book may be reproduced or transmitted in any form or by any means without written permission from the author.

Scripture quotations from HOLY BIBLE: NEW INTERNATIONAL VERSION®. ©1973, 1978, 1984, by International Bible Society. Used by permission of Zondervan Publishing House. All rights reserved.

ISBN-13: 978-1505356168

Printed in USA by CreateSpace (www.CreateSpace.com)

Dedication

This book is dedicated to my wife and best friend, Jennifer. Your support and encouragement are beyond words. Thanks also to the five Willis young men. Caleb, Micah, Josiah, Gabriel, and Luke. You are each a blessing. I love you, my family!

A huge "Thank you" to Matt Smith, your willingness to meet with me and mark up my drafts were a great encouragement to me during this writing project. I look forward to many years spurring one another on in our writing efforts. "BOOM!"

Finally, to the men and women in the trenches of ministry leadership at Bent Tree Bible Fellowship. You have answered a call to pour yourself into the lives of others. Many of whom invite you into very painful places. May these words of wisdom find a place near your heart:

"…He who refreshes others will himself be refreshed." – Proverbs 11:25b (NIV)

Table of Contents

Foreword 5
Preface 6
Introduction 7
January 9
February 14
March 21
April 28
May 35
June 40
July 47
August 54
September 61
October 68
November 75
December 78

Foreword

As I type the word "Foreword", I am reminded of the word "Forward". What are you looking forward to as you hold this book? What are you anticipating in this coming year? My prayer is that you will be reminded every month of your amazing calling to leadership.

For the past 24 years, I have had the privilege of being married to Eric. He has an incredible gift for encouraging leaders, pastors, and missionaries to stay the course. But you cannot truly minister out of an empty heart. We both know the need for Christian leaders to find "Breathing Space" in their worlds.

We have learned the hard lessons of living life without margin and without taking time to be still, regroup, refresh, and recharge. There will always be more demands on you than can fit in your planner. My prayer is that you will make "Breathing Space" a priority.

The following chapters flow from Eric's heart – his attempt to help you navigate the difficult and beautiful journey of ministry. May God truly bless your coming year and remind you of His immeasurable love for you.

Looking forward,

Jennifer Willis
Wife of Eric and mother of their five sons

Preface

I'm sitting in my favorite chair surrounded by bookshelves filled with a blend of fiction, poetry, non-fiction, and a picture book or two. It's one of my happy places. To make it truly happy, give me a Rocky Mountain view with a hot cup of coffee and I'm lost for hours. You have one of those places, right? A place where you can escape the chaos and find a small sliver of solace?

Ministry leadership takes its toll and we need to pull away from the hectic pace of daily challenges to refocus and rekindle the fire of our passion. Just reading those words has a tendency to put a tight grip in the chest. To know we need to replenish our souls is one thing; to actually do it is quite another. Many of us have tried to do both; staying in the trenches of ministry leadership while hoping daily doses of limited minutes in God's Word will keep us fresh. Have you ever been thirsty? I mean throat dry, about to die, thirsty? Trying to lead while taking small amounts of spiritual nourishment along the way is like back breaking work on a hot summer day with only a cup of tap water to make it through. The ration is too small to sustain the long day. How far into the day before you long for a deluge of cold water, not only for your thirst, but to pour over your drained, sweaty, aching body?

Over the course of the next twelve months, I'm inviting you on a journey; a spiritual pilgrimage of sorts. The pages ahead will meander through the calendar at a pace that quickens the heart yet stills the soul. Like a refreshing glass of cold water as you go about your painstakingly hot work, let this book be an oasis. Consider it a monthly respite, *Breathing Space* to immerse yourself in Living Water.

Introduction

To use this resource well, view it as a workbook. Write in its pages, mark in its margins and let your pen reveal the thread of God's redemptive story in your life. Each chapter is devoted to one of the calendar months.

This is not a daily devotional, it's a monthly retreat. Take your calendar before it reaches capacity and choose one day each month to commit a six hour block of uninterrupted time away. Take this day to find a place in solitude beneficial for hanging out with your Creator: You, your Bible, this workbook and pen.

You'll be prompted for responses and given the opportunity to capture what God's Word has shown you. Let me encourage you not to gloss over the questions or speed read the verses that may be overly familiar. This day is intentional space for you and your Lord to walk, talk, and simply be with one another.

For each of your 12 days away this year, consider this formula for preparation:

Two weeks before, secure your retreat location. Your office does not qualify as a "retreat location" so try to be a bit more creative.

One week before, it's a great time to get your prayer warriors around you! Contact at least 3 people whom will commit to pray for you on your day away. (*With* you before the retreat and *for* you on the day of your retreat).

One week before and up until the day of, send us an email letting us know what day you're headed out for some *Breathing Space*. You can do that through www.ReclaimLeadership.org. We'll be praying!

Night before, if married, handwrite a note to your spouse with specific gratitude for their support of you and the ministry. If this is a difficult note to write or a difficult note for your spouse to receive, contact Eric@ReclaimLeadership.org to set a time for a call of prayer and encouragement.

Day of, start with stillness, silence, no electronics, unplug and be present in your environment. Pray and allow the Lord to meet you in the midst of your processing the questions and Scripture you'll find in this book.

Night of or day after, share what your time away with God produced in your heart, affirmed in your relationships, or solidified in your direction. www.ReclaimLeadership.org We will celebrate with you!

> Enjoy the journey! Take your *Breathing Space* and do just that...
> ...breathe.

JANUARY

It's that time of year when we are so excited for what could be! But wait. Allow your thoughts to go in reverse and recover the past year: The work, the people, the events that defined your life. As you look back over the past twelve months, what do you see? Your calendar was full with appointments, breakfast meetings, counseling sessions, celebrations and walking lonely corridors of the grieving heart. You poured yourself out in ministry. What made last year successful? What are you measuring to determine if what you did made a difference in another person's life? Can you put a face to those individuals whose souls were allowed to cross your path? Do you recall the life transformations? Can you celebrate a new life in Christ? After all, January is a time to think "new".

There have been many opportunities this past year for you to be used by God in the lives of other people as He has accomplished His work in them. Celebrate those moments! Be reminded of Paul's words to the Corinthian believers in his letter to them:

"You yourselves are our letter, written on our hearts, known and read by everybody. You show that you are a letter from Christ, the result of ministry, written not with ink but with the Spirit of the living God, not on tablets of stone but on tablets of human hearts."
2 Corinthians 3:2-3 (NIV)

It's incredible to think about having a profound influence on someone's spiritual life. That's exactly where the following reflections are intended to take you.

Last year I began with a dream, a goal, a mission and purpose to invest in the lives of others by:

I sensed myself becoming overwhelmed this past year when this situation, this person, or my perceptions took me to that place. It seemed hopeless, yet I leaned heavily into Christ and saw him use me in this way:

In my humble submission allowing Christ to serve through me this past year, I learned this about my God, His story, His mercies:

God's Word in context of 2 Corinthians 3:2-3 has shown me…

FEBRUARY

Love is a wonderful thing!

You've taught with three points and illustrations about God's love. You may have studied the Greek and can eloquently speak the words that capture love. Speaking and showing are day and night. They are their most beautiful when they meet. Sunrise, Sunset. You're here now with God on the topic of love. Better still, you're here now with Love! You are most beautiful when you're with Him.

The Apostle John wrote a series of 3 short letters captured in Scripture. His first Epistle gives us this incredible reminder:

"This is how God showed his love among us; He sent his one and only Son into the world that we might live through him. This is love: not that we loved God, but that he loved us and sent his Son as an atoning sacrifice for our sins. Dear friends, since God so loved us, we also ought to love one another. No one has ever seen God; but if we love one another, God lives in us and his love is made complete in us. We know that we live in him and he in us, because he has given us of his Spirit." 1 John 4:9-13 (NIV)

Thank God for his love and express your heart toward him:

How do I share God's love with the people closest to me? With those acquaintances who cross my path?

In what ways has my lacking love for God kept me from fully enjoying his call to minister? When have I experienced great joy because of his indwelling love ministering through me?

I worship God out of genuine love when I remember:

To live in the love God has provided me, requires me to make changes in the following areas:

God's Word in context of 1 John 4:9-13 has shown me…

MARCH

Don't forget to wear green on a specific day this month or the most unluckiness of bad luck will fall on you! Luck... What exactly is that? For centuries, the term was used to define the good or bad circumstances in which people found themselves. In modern times, it has morphed to encompass a pseudo-spiritual essence one can wish upon themselves or others.

Ultimately, luck is the term we use when we refuse to acknowledge the hand of God. His sovereignty over and in all things of life is easily overlooked as we flippantly throw life into the realm of luck.

The Apostle Peter directed his second letter as a warning to believers against false prophets who came with good sounding arguments but whose message flew in the face of the true Gospel:

"But there were also false prophets among the people, just as there will be false teachers among you. They will secretly introduce destructive heresies, even denying the sovereign Lord who bought them—bringing swift destruction on themselves. Many will follow their shameful ways and will bring the way of truth into disrepute." 2 Peter 2:1-2 (NIV)

Where have I attempted to give credence to luck in circumstances when in fact the hand of God was moving?

How do I define God's sovereignty?

Where have I seen or sensed God moving in my life situations?

I anticipate and desperately desire God to move in the following areas:

In order to realign my thoughts with His, I must:

God's Word in context of 2 Peter 2:1-2 has shown me…

APRIL

"April showers bring may flowers" There's a joke there about the pilgrims, but I digress.

Showers, rain pouring down bring nourishment to the ground producing some of the most magnificent of changes. Have you breathed the fresh air after an April shower? It has a cleansing purpose. The stale is washed away, the new is being birthed.

Let your heavenly Father's rain of Grace fall anew on you. Where is the stale that needs refreshing? Are you harboring bitterness disguised as righteous piety? Have you justified holding onto something that needs washing; either cleansed to make new or washed away altogether?

Timothy had a great mentor in the Apostle Paul. The mentor's words of encouragement to lead spiritually are words for us today:

"In a large house there are articles not only of gold and silver, but also of wood and clay; some are for noble purposes and some for ignoble. If a man cleanses himself from the latter, he will be an instrument for noble purposes, made holy, useful to the Master and prepared to do any good work." 2 Timothy 2:20-21 (NIV)

What areas of my life are needlessly hindering my expression of the fullness of Christ in me?

Write a prayer asking The Lord to reveal, refresh, and renew you today…

What areas of my life are fully surrendered as an instrument for noble purposes, set apart as holy, and useful to the Master?

How will I nurture my soul on a regular basis?

To whom and how will I share the joy of my salvation?

God's Word in context of 2 Timothy 2:20-21 has shown me…

MAY

Finished something lately? Thousands of people are finishing a journey this month… their formal education. Remember your graduation? High school, college, maybe even seminary? Oh the euphoria of accomplishment and finality of being done!

You and I both know that was only the beginning. Our true education began the moment our formal education came to an end. What have you learned lately? It's said that "leaders are readers" and "leaders never stop growing". Leaders are learners.

The Jewish Rabbinical system placed great emphasis on learning. The Pharisees and Sadducees of Jesus' time were extremely learned men. Rabbi's would hand pick their students by observing their intellectual abilities and asking them to follow in order to learn from them. Sitting at the Rabbi's feet to glean the wisdom taught.

Jesus radically patronized that system when he stirred the hearts of twelve common, intellectually dull men with the invitation to follow him. He then opened the invitation for those who would believe on him. In red letters of Scripture:

"Come to me, all you who are weary and burdened, and I will give you rest. Take my yoke upon you and learn from me, for I am gentle and humble in heart, and you will find rest for your souls. For my yoke is easy and my burden is light." Matthew 11:28-30 (NIV)

How am I continuing to educate myself in ministry? Am I searching to sit at the feet of the latest theologian or am I intentionally learning at the feet of Jesus?

What rhythm of learning works best for me? Daily, monthly, annually. What does this look like?

What is Jesus teaching me for growing in knowledge, understanding, and application of my:

Personal character?

Ministry skills?

Spiritual gifts?

God's Word in context of Matthew 11:28-30 has shown me…

JUNE

Where did this year go? I need a vacation! Summer has come and it's time to play. You were made to play; a frolicking, fun kind of play. God likes to see us taking time to enjoy the fruit of our labors. Or does He? Is there ever such a thing as a ministry leader on vacation? What is a vacation anyway? Away time, down time, family time, it is time not spent in the usual but rather invested in the opposite.

With the notion of vacation comes the guilt of taking a reprieve from the daily tasks of ministry. Get over it! Rest is biblical. In seminary, I was required to read the book "*When I Relax, I Feel* Guilty" by Tim Hansel. You may want to pick up a copy!

Reality check: You are a minister of the Gospel of Jesus Christ. Your title or position doesn't make you a minister. You are just as much an Ambassador for Christ when your body is toasting on sandy beaches as when you're frocked in front of a congregation. The difference is in the application of sacerdotal duties. Temporarily pull back from the task, not the faith!

The author of Hebrews (whomever you're inclined to note as its Holy Spirit empowered author) shared wise words for us to heed:

"There remains then, a Sabbath-rest for the people of God; for anyone who enters God's rest also rests form his own work, just as God did from his. Let us, therefore, make every effort to enter that rest, so that no one will fall by following their example of disobedience." Hebrews 4:9-11 (NIV)

Recalling my last intentional break from ministry routine, what about my time away was invigorating or healing?

What steps do I take to make sure ministry continues once I take a reprieve? How will my flock be shepherded in my short absence?

How long does it usually take me to "detox" and unplug my mind from the rigors of ministry in order to enjoy time away? How can I make that transition easier?

If I've not taken a vacation this year, what am I planning for intentional rest? If I have already vacationed this year, what will I do differently to make it more restful?

Write a prayer of thanksgiving to God for the benefit of His rest and a commitment to pursue it.

God's Word in context of Hebrews 4:9-11 shows me…

JULY

Freedom is the theme that gets all the attention this month. You are free! It's true for the individual living in the United States and it's just as true for those believers living under tyranny! Freedom is not a political position, it's a spiritual condition.

As we celebrate our nation's independence, consider the freedom you have in Christ.

Some of us have lived in freedom so long that we have no concept of what it is to be hopelessly entangled, captured with no resource of our own to grant us independence. How long have you lived in the freedom of Christ? Long enough to have forgotten the chains of spiritual slavery that lay near us each day? The shackles have been destroyed and yet like the elephant who was chained at birth and trained to his limitations, you have remained in the imaginary shackles bound to a limited experience of God's amazing freedom.

The Roman Empire of Paul's day found many Gentiles searching after the one true God. Paul wrote these new converts as they gathered in synagogues across the empire to teach them theological truths of their new found faith in Christ.

"If we have been united with him (Christ) like this in his death, we will certainly also be united with him in his resurrection. For we know that our old self was crucified with him so that the body of sin might be done away with, that we should no longer be slaves to sin—because anyone who has died has been freed from sin." Romans 6:5-7 (NIV)

What words, pictures, or phrases capture my thoughts on the freedom I have in Christ?

What hinders me from living in the freedom I have in Christ?

What role does God's Grace play in my ability to live in that freedom?

How am I celebrating my freedom in front of others still in the chains of spiritual slavery?

What does it look like for freedom to permeate my thoughts, feelings, and choices?

God's Word in context of Romans 6:5-7 shows me…

AUGUST

The summer doldrums are here. It seems everything moves slower in the doldrums. It's a nautical term. It's measurable. That's what makes it scientific. No winds to fill the sails. No sailing in the doldrums. Floating. Bobbing. Sitting. Waiting. Simply not moving forward. Your soul experiences doldrums as well. Not in the nautical science sense, but nonetheless real. Downcast, depressed, lethargic.

Ministry leaders I routinely coach find themselves struggling with their emotions. Along with that struggle comes the added self-inflicted spiritual abuse of thinking they are faithless in their emotional muck. It's time to right size your understanding of those seasons of low points in your life.

It was an ancient dilemma of commoners and kings. God in his desire to relate to mankind, allowed King David to write for the director of music. A maskil of the Sons of Korah. A song whose words are rich with the emotions of all.

"My tears have been my food day and night, while men say to me all day long, 'where is your God?' These things I remember as I pour out my soul: how I used to go with the multitude, leading the procession to the house of God, with shouts of joy and thanksgiving among the festive throng. Why are you downcast, O my soul? Why so disturbed within me? Put your hope in God, for I will yet praise him, my Savior and my God." Psalm 42:3-5 (NIV)

Are my emotions healthy? How do I define healthy emotions? What do I consider as unhealthy emotions?

What can I identify as events or circumstances that seem to pull me into feeling low? Who are the people to whom I find it difficult to minister? How do I allow them to affect me?

How often do I find myself in a place of not moving forward? When the emotional doldrums hit, how have I historically found myself "floating, bobbing, sitting, and waiting" them out?

How can the truth of my identity in Christ influence my thoughts and actions when I find myself in a low emotional season?

What would I like to do differently when faced with emotional lows? The next time I find myself lamenting in anguish, I plan to…

God's Word in context of Psalm 42:3-5 shows me…

SEPTEMBER

Depending on where you live, September brings an acquittal from the summer heat! Fall brings such a rush of hopeful anticipation. Harvest time is near. What will the garden produce this year? Harvest time.

Remember when our society was one based on agriculture? Me neither. However, we are still in the AG business as believers. Preparing fields to plant seed, watering, and reaping a harvest of the spiritual.

You and I both know the Lord is the one who draws people to himself through the work of the Holy Spirit. Does this knowledge cause you to be lax in your desire to have spiritual conversations with others or does it embolden you to seek such opportunities?

The journal of a doctor captured the moment when Jesus appointed and sent seventy-two of his followers into the spiritual fields for harvest.

"He (Jesus) told them, 'The harvest is plentiful, but the workers are few. Ask the Lord of the harvest, therefore, to send out workers ino his harvest field. Go! I am sending you out like lambs among wolves…" Luke 10:2-3 (NIV)

What have I planted spiritually in the previous months or years that I can't wait to come to fruition?

What part of the spiritual harvest (planting, watering, harvesting) is the most natural for me? Which is more difficult? How do I view the harvesting process?

Write a fictitious dialogue where you engage a person in a spiritual conversation.

Who in my life acted as spiritual farmers to plant, water, and reap my soul? Write a note of thanks for what God did through those individuals.

Take a look back to page 56. Remember those people? Pray a blessing over each of them individually and write a prayer of thanksgiving for what God taught you through your encounters with them.

God's Word in context of Luke 10:2-3 shows me…

OCTOBER

Pull out the sweaters and turtlenecks. Winter is on the way! Clothing yourself in warmer gear is a necessity for the majority of people living in cooler climates. Boxes come out of closets and clothes are exchanged in each. Away with the shorts and tank tops, in with the wool socks. How's your wardrobe fairing?

Scripture teaches us to put off and put on. Take the old and put it away in order to put on the new. The Apostle Paul's instructions to the church in Colossae laid out specific rules for holy living. These rules are actually representations of the choices you and I have on a daily basis. Choices to be influenced by the flesh or by the Spirit. Scripture lists characteristics of both in several places. But today, take time to read Colossians 3:1-17.

Begin your time there this month and consider your spiritual wardrobe. If you're artistically inclined, feel free to draw a picture here of the wardrobe that fills your spiritual closet.

What do I understand about the biblical counsel of putting off and putting on?

How do these concepts play out in my daily life?

Looking back, what did I exchange for Christ's new life?

Looking at the present, what needs to be put off in order for me to live fully in Christ's new life?

Looking forward, what can I identify as spiritual benchmarks that will affirm my putting on the spiritual things of God?

God's Word in context of Colossians 3:1-17 shows me…

NOVEMBER

"Thank you" One of the simplest of expressions.

"Enter his gates with thanksgiving and his courts with praise; give thanks to him and praise his name. For the LORD is good and his love endures forever; his faithfulness continues through all generations." - Psalm 100:4-5 (NIV)

Now it's your turn to write a psalm to God. Enter his gates with thanksgiving in your own words from your own heart, thank God for the difficulties, turmoil, and challenges of this past year.

Write a note of "Thanks" to the person(s) who have supported your ministry by allowing you the Breathing Space to take a respite.

God's Word in context of Psalm 100 shows me…

DECEMBER

One birth above all other births! It's Jesus! He's here… he's actually here! But wait… according to our society, that news is old. It's now a season of gift giving off of wish lists while we tell stories about a round jolly guy in a red suit.

Make sure your finances are in order because the more kids you have, the more the budget takes a hit. The reality of the season has us walking that line of revering the holy and haggling deals with retailers.

The ultimate gift to mankind is overlooked at worst and underwhelmed at best. But the Christmas season is not Christ's only coming. The Gift once born for salvation will once again come to earth fulfilling God's redemptive covenant.

John was shown on the Isle of Patmos what he wrote in utter awe as the ultimate gift awaiting the believer.

"The Spirit and the bride say, 'Come!' And let him who hears say, 'Come!' Whoever is thirsty, let him come; and whoever wishes, let him take the free gift of the water of life." –Revelation 22:17 (NIV)

What meaning do I attach to getting both the Christmas gift of salvation and the Coming gift of living water?

How have I (in what areas) have I been slow to come to Him?

Write a note to convey your anticipation of our coming Lord…

God's Word in context of Revelation 22:17 shows me…

CONGRATULATIONS!

You completed a journey of intentional self-care in ministry. May you sense the real presence of the incredible Power of the Indwelling Christ!

What will you do with what you've experienced? Look back over your responses to find those which prompted action. Now lean into The Lord for courage and boldness to move in the direction that most honors and glorifies God.

Eric is available to coach you through the wonderful and sometimes treacherous journey of ministry. You can contact him by visiting www.ReclaimLeadership.org.

God bless you as He blesses His ministry through you!

45660308R00048

Made in the USA
Charleston, SC
01 September 2015